# MAN

## Pat Kennett

WORLD TRUCKS NO 4

ts
**TRANSPORTATION SERIES**

**AZTEX CORPORATION**
7002 E. PASEO SAN ANDRES
TUCSON, ARIZONA 85710

AZTEX CORPORATION

Also in the same series and by the same author

**No 1 : ERF**
**No 2 : Scania**
**No 3 : Seddon Atkinson**
**No 5 : DAF**
**No 6 : Dennis**

First published in 1978

Printed in Great Britain
Library of Congress Catalog Card Number 78-61461
ISBN 0-89404-015-4

# CONTENTS

# AUTHOR'S PREFACE

In researching this, the fourth volume in the *World Trucks* series, it was necessary to go right back to the middle of the 19th century when the German industrial revolution was still in full swing. When a company is as old as that a certain amount of legend accumulates over the years, particularly about the earlier events. In this book I have tried to put aside such legend and in its place select hard facts to outline the early progress of the company. Another difficulty with a company like MAN is that its structure is large and complex and the activities of one part — in this case the commercial vehicle section — are difficult to separate from the whole. However, I have tried to concentrate on the vehicles as far as possible, without ignoring the great breadth of engineering enterprise encompassed by MAN.

A great deal of help was given by the Deutsches Museum in the writing of this book and any visitor to Munich should really treat himself to a visit to this treasure house of the past, nestling on the banks of the Isar river. He will not be disappointed, and much of the display information is given in English. I should also record the enormous amount of help given by my good friend Egon Bode of MAN's Export Department who helped to co-ordinate my researches within the company and opened the right doors in that huge and rather complex organisation.

MAN's history is inextricably tied up with the work of Dr Diesel and it is regrettable that only a short summary of his efforts can be included here as so much of what we nowadays expect from our trucks can be traced directly back to his work with compression ignition technology. However MAN engineers translated much of that work into usuable technology and that story forms a vital part of this book, which makes this volume rather different from the others in the series as it involves the history of the whole industry and not just one manufacturer.

Pat Kennett

# MAN BECOMES MOBILE

Gebrüder Schultheiß Ziegeleiwarenfabrik
Spardorf - Erlangen
Telefon 50

The origins of the giant engineering group called MAN — thankfully short for the Maschinenfabrik Augsburg-Nürnberg Aktiengesellschaft — go back to the very beginnings of the industrial revolution itself in central Europe. That revolution came rather later in Germany than it did in Britain, for the very good reason that almost a century of squabbling and political manoeuvring had kept what is now called Germany very fragmented until about 1848. Neither did the European countries have the wealth of talent and inventiveness at that period that the great Victorian engineers had given Britain.

At the time it was commonplace to find British engineering enterprise and expertise at almost every turn in Europe and further afield. The Lancashire engineer Edward Earnshaw had provided steam engines in many factories including Nürnberg gas works, while Joseph Cockerill had built the massive steam propulsion engines for the biggest Rhine ship at the time, the *Germania* built in 1841. James Watt himself was well known in those parts too, having installed a number of his pumping engines in Bavaria at the very beginning of the 19th century. It was not that the British were necessarily better craftsmen, it was merely that while much of Europe embroiled itself in political and territorial wranglings, Queen Victoria's engineers got peacefully on with their tasks.

Bavaria, which comprises the south-eastern region of Germany, was in the early and mid-19th century an independent state, with a history of culture and commerce of the highest standards. Old cities like Nürnberg, Würzburg and Augsburg that had once been thriving merchant centres on the 'romantic highway' down through Europe, followed by the traders between the Baltic, the North Sea and the Mediterranean, had slowly regressed into quiet cultural centres while it was Munich that provided most of the limited industrial activity of Bavaria. International trade routes had gone westward as America became more and more important. But if the towns were slowly going to sleep, certain of their inhabitants were not. The growth and prosperity brought about by industrialisation in Britain was like a beckoning light to some far-thinking citizens. And the new mobility of the railways for both people and goods was envied not only in Bavaria but throughout central Europe.

A prominent Nürnberg merchant by the name of Johann Friedrich Klett became very interested in a new railway project that was being discussed in his city in 1835, and in fact it was his brother-in-law, Johann Platner, who became head of the new railway company. A great deal of ridicule was poured on the whole scheme, but the Klett family were made of stern stuff, and they pressed ahead. Klett decided that the best chance of getting it right was to find the best experts available. He and Platner approached George Stephenson as their original consultant, though he did not produce any detailed engineering work. A civil engineer, Paul Dennis, who had been working in Munich was engaged to look after the track, earthworks and bridges, while the chief locomotive and rolling stock engineer was a man called William Wilson, who brought the two original locomotives, *Adler* and *Pfeil* (*Eagle* and *Arrow*) over from England.

Together with local skills and labour the Ludwigsbahn railway was completed by the early summer of 1836. The line was a mere five kilometres long, but the new means of transport captured the imagination of all Bavaria. The railway revolution was suddenly a fact, and the magic of engineering was by now in Klett's blood. In 1841 he established a small engineering plant in Nürnberg itself. There was opposition to such a move, with claims from the populace that 'his furnaces would disturb their work and their sleep, and the sparks would set light to the hay wagons', but that didn't last long when it was seen how new jobs and prosperity would result. Just how fast that plant grew can be seen by the fact that within 12 years, orders for 1000 or more railway trucks at a time were being placed. The firm was still known as Klett & Comp, but by 1871 it became known as the Maschinenbau AG, Nürnberg, providing the M and the N in the eventual title of MAN. By that time it was Theodor Cramer Klett who was in charge of the factory, and his visions of energy were, if anything, greater than those of his father-in-law, Johann. A statue of Theodor stands outside the Nürnberg works to this day, and indeed many local folk still refer to the factory as 'Cramer Klett's' rather than by its official MAN title.

While all that was going on, one Ludwig Sander had established a small machine shop in the town of Augsburg in 1840. He had no spectacular railway to launch his activity, but he still had the wrath of the townsfolk to contend with as had most industrialists at the time. But whereas in Nürnberg the emphasis was on structures and rolling stock, the theme at Augsburg was power supply, or to be more specific, steam power. Augsburg-built engines were supplied to many of Germany's major breweries, as well as an immense variety of other manufacturing plants from fabric mills to paint factories. By 1857, after various management changes, it became known as the Maschinenfabrik Augsburg AG — the eventual A in MAN. But although there was a considerable amount of co-operation between the two, it was not until 1898 that a formal merger was made and the group became known as the Vereinigte Maschinenfabrik Augsburg und Maschinenbaugesellschaft Nürnberg Aktiengesellschaft! Ten years later, to the undoubted relief of the company clerks, that was shortened to the present title Maschinenfabrik Augsburg-Nürnberg AG, known simply as MAN.

By that time the group was already very large. There were factories at Gustavsberg on the Rhine, which originated as a construction camp for bridges being built there, at Hamburg where marine engine installations were carried out for shipbuilders, and at Munich where a branch company had been formed to carry out a great deal of the constructional work. This included some of Germany's most spectacular railway bridges and Germany's own Crystal Palace, built in Munich in 1854, just three years after the one in London and similarly constructed entirely in cast iron and glass.

Large as the MAN group was, it was matched by a number of other engineering combines in Germany and was by no means unique. What made it so different eventually was the work of one man who many regarded as something of a crank. The name of that man was Rudolf Diesel. His work placed MAN in a unique position and changed the whole course of power generation engineering.

Rudolf Diesel was born in Paris in 1858 and attended technical college in Munich to be lectured by, among others, Carl Linde who was a renowned steam engine and refrigeration engineer with connections at MAN. He also had frequent contact with Heinrich Buz, MAN's works director. Diesel was an accomplished linguist as well as a talented engineer, and his involvement with industrial activities became closer when he was asked to act as interpreter on a tour made by Linde throughout Europe to study and discuss engines, pumps and refrigeration. One thing young Diesel learned was that steam engines made poor use of the potential energy that was put into them; in other words their thermal efficiency was low. At the age of 34 he had done enough theoretical work to have the confidence to ask Heinrich Buz if he could come to Augsburg to try and develop an engine that would run on crude oil, ignited by the heat of compression alone. The internal combustion engine invented by N.A. Otto in Germany was already being manufactured in Germany by Carl Benz and Gottlieb Daimler and others elsewhere, including Crossley in England, while an oil-fuelled engine had been designed and run in Britain as early as 1890, and production engines were installed from 1892, made by Hornsby's of Grantham for the designer Herbert Ackroyd-Stuart.

The Hornsby-Ackroyd engines worked by injecting gas oil into a small pre-combustion chamber before expanding into the main cylinder. Diesel wanted to build an engine where the fuel was injected directly into the cylinder. It would, he reasoned, give a higher thermal efficiency than any other engine known and he took out a patent in February 1892. His theory was correct but hard to achieve in practice. Buz had sufficient acumen to see that if it succeeded, Diesel's idea would revolutionise the power business, and he readily gave his consent for Diesel to start work. In the spring of 1893 Rudolf Diesel began to tackle the problems of putting theory into practice. Although he did the work at the Augsburg MAN factory, he had his office and home in Munich, and leading technicians from all over Germany were frequent visitors to his rooms, such was the interest in his work. It took four years to build a successful engine that would run continuously. One prototype refused to run at all, and the second for short periods only. The design was nothing like the diesel engine we know today, but modelled on contemporary gas and steam engine construction, with heavier parts to withstand the higher pressures involved. Despite its enormous size — 3.5 metres high exclusive of the flywheel in the pit below — the engine developed a modest 20 horsepower at 172 rpm. But the important thing was that it worked, and it worked by injecting fuel directly into the cylinder. Its thermal efficiency was 27 per cent, at least half as much again as any other engine, and nearly three times as much as a steam unit.

That fuel injection was not like modern injection, nor indeed like that on the Hornsby-Ackroyd engine, but relied on a blast of air from a compressor to carry fuel into the cylinder, which of course already contained compressed and heated air. The effect of that 'blast injection' as it was called, was to raise the temperature a little higher and atomise the fuel, which would then burn slowly and smoothly. The fuel itself was a light crude oil, more like kerosene than the diesel oil we know today, and of course was very cheap at that time. The success of that engine was widely acclaimed because of Diesel's connections throughout industry, and in 1898 four engines were built for exhibition and demonstration purposes. Two of these were made in the MAN plants at Nürnberg and Augsburg, one by Krupps at Düsseldorf, and one by the Deutz gas engine company at Cologne. The two Nürnberg engines later spent some time generating electrical power in Munich.

Although Diesel did all his development and original construction at MAN, and his first engines could be legitimately called MAN products, it was to Deutz that he turned for subsequent commercial development of his invention, leaving MAN somewhat churlishly aside. The problem with the diesel was that it worked well in big sizes — Deutz made numerous examples with about 125 horsepower per cylinder — where the injector was about 30 cm long, but it stubbornly refused to work in scaled down versions. As the 20th century dawned, Rudolf Diesel saw his invention working efficiently in considerable numbers, but far too big and heavy to be used as a motive power unit, which was one of the aims he had discussed with Buz. Little did he know, at that time, what the impact of his invention was to be on the road transport industry. But although Diesel himself departed, his work lived on at Augsburg, and Buz saw to it that a steady programme of engine development proceeded. By 1901 he had a four-stroke engine producing 70 horsepower at 160 rpm, and by 1904 his first 'high-speed' engine which ran at 400 rpm to produce 140 horsepower. Six years later big marine diesels with reversible crankshafts to eliminate external gearing were being built with up to 850 horsepower from six cylinders. But all that was getting the road transport application nowhere.

Sadly, Rudolf Diesel did not survive to enjoy the fruits of his labours. A series of attacks on him by intellectuals in various German universities during the early years of the century, concerning allegations that his patent did not entirely tally with his actual design, made him depressed and he invariably sought solitude. That he made a successful engine while his opponents did not, does not seem to have entered into the arguments. Eventually in 1913 after a particularly vicious attack on him was published, he disappeared overboard from a cross-Channel steamer, and the great man was lost for ever.

\* \* \*

Vast though the engineering enterprises of the MAN concern were, it was the enthusiasm of Anton Rieppel, the works director at Nürnberg, which brought about MAN's entry into the motor vehicle field. Heinrich Buz at Augsburg liked the Diesel concept but saw it mainly as an industrial engine. Rieppel on the other hand was convinced that the engine had enormous potential as a motive power unit, not only for waggons or lorries, but for trams, railway cars and other relatively small vehicles like farm tractors. He could see transport costs mounting even then, and a power source using cheap fuel was bound to succeed in the end, he argued. He was proved to be quite right but he had a long time to wait. He was in fact building what he called 'coach engines' as early as 1899, but these worked on the Otto principle rather than Diesel's. Over the next few years Rieppel built numerous small engines for industrial and marine purposes, always with a road vehicle application at the back of his mind. But it was not until 1914 that he managed to convince his board of directors that the road freight lorry was a business into which MAN might profitably venture. Even then, it was a licensing agreement with the established Swiss firm of Adolf Saurer that marked the beginnings of MAN as vehicle builders.

It is significant that even at that very early date in automobile engineering history MAN decided on a rationalised construction system similar in principle to that used today in their heavy trucks. The four-cylinder engine design was by Saurer, but the Nürnberg engineers examined it and decided that they could produce three versions using the same basic components, and indeed the idea was successful. Using a common cylinder bore of 85 mm and three different strokes of 140 mm, 160 mm and 180 mm, three different power outputs of 30, 36, and 45 horsepower were available. Not only that, but the longer relative stroke of the larger engines gave them torque outputs that were proportionally higher than the short-stroke types, which made them doubly suitable for the heavy lorry applications that they were intended to fulfil. Iron cylinder blocks were cast in pairs and bolted to an aluminium crankcase. The engineers within the group already had adequate experience of transmission systems for industrial uses, so they designed and built their own four-speed gearbox for the trucks too. Lighter machines had a shaft drive to a live rear axle, but the heavier ones had a countershaft across the rear of the gearbox, from which chains drove the rear wheels. The chassis began as a copy of the existing Saurer design, but steadily grew away from that pattern with the addition of better springing, riveted construction instead of bolts, and stiffer frame members.

The initial model range was announced in 1915 and prototypes built that year, but it was not until 1916 that full production became available. Rieppel was ecstatic. He now had every reason to step up research on his beloved direct injection oil engine and make it suitable for vehicular use. Meanwhile the trucks were immediately accepted on the market, and steady production of up to ten chassis a week was common during 1916.

The basic truck range comprised four models all with a choice of engines as detailed below.

This range of weight capacities and engines was quite unusual at that time and the MAN became widely used both for military purposes and in industry. It proved to be a sturdy and reliable machine too, and although fuel supply problems occurred during the 1914-18 hostilities, the engines proved capable of running on a wide variety of fuels from good quality kerosene and benzine to industrial alcohol, or any mixture of these. Of course, in those days, emissions were not a matter of public concern, which is just as well under the circumstances! Before long optional equipment made the chassis extremely well equipped by truck standards, with self-starters, speedometers, central chassis lubrication and an exhaust brake. Like almost all heavy vehicles of its period, the MAN had brakes on the rear wheels only, with an emergency 'sprag' that could be dropped from the back of the chassis to prevent running back on a hill. There was a transmission park brake too, but from all accounts that was not the best part of the truck! All the early trucks had hickory-wood wheels, with solid tyres, although within two years, the heavier machines began to be fitted with cast steel wheels and the lighter ones with pneumatic tyres. Like the early Scanias in Sweden, the MANs all had wheels mounted on ball bearings.

Within 12 months of the first truck chassis

appearing, modified versions built specially for bus operation were announced. These used the same engine and transmission arrangements, but the chassis were slung rather lower, on softer springs and had the fuel tank moved to the extreme rear of the chassis. The bus models were based on the two and three tonner chassis with identical track and wheelbases. Bodywork in great variety was offered, much of it actually built by MAN rather than outside bodybuilders. Standard bus bodies had seats for 21 passengers on the smaller chassis, and 28 on the bigger version. There were also a number of double-deck buses built, as early as 1916, and these carried between 36 and 42 passengers, according to the wishes of the operators who bought them. Several city authorities used these double deckers, including Nürnberg itself, while other MANs could be found as far away as Hamburg and Cologne.

Apart from standard body designs, a great variety of special types were built on MAN chassis by proprietary coach-builders, both for freight and passenger use. Fire engines, furniture vans, tankers, refuse trucks, post buses, ambulances, tower wagons (for maintaining tram overhead cables), insulated meat vans, open-topped charabancs, all came in this category. There was one experimental fire engine with all-wheel-drive built in about 1916, but as no further trace of the design emerges after that, one can only assume that it was unsuccessful.

The basic truck and bus chassis design was so successful as a concept that it continued with only minor changes well into the 1920s, although the truck models were continued long after newer bus designs were developed. Better materials were used following the cessation of hostilities. For example, all axles were made from extremely tough nickel-chrome steel from 1921 onwards, and tougher aluminium alloys were used for the engine crankcases. A great deal of research was done on braking methods and materials, and MAN touring coaches had a nationwide reputation for safety and comfort by the early 1920s. But all those detailed technical developments, creditable though they were, were overshadowed by a much more important technical breakthrough. That was the automotive diesel engine.

| Type | Two tonner | Three tonner | Four tonner | Five tonner |
|---|---|---|---|---|
| Payload capacity | 2000 kg | 3500 kg | 4000-4300 kg | 5000 kg |
| Engine choice | 30, 36, 45 hp | 30, 36, 45 hp | 30, 36, 45 hp | 36, 45 hp |
| Drive system | Shaft/live axle | Shaft/live axle | Countershaft/chains | Countershaft/chains |
| Maximum speed | 30 kph (19 mph) | 30 kph (19 mph) | 24 kph (15 mph) | 18 kph (12 mph) |
| Unladen weight with body | 2700-2900 kg | 3100-3350 kg | 3250-3550 kg | 3800-4100 kg |
| Tyre size front/rear | 870-100/955-100 | 870-110/975-120 | 900-120/1060-120 | 900-130/1050-140 |

Rudolf Diesel's patent for his 'oil burning machine' was taken out in 1892. Despite success of his work, he was pilloried for years by engineering intellectuals who maintained that his engines did not comply with the patent.

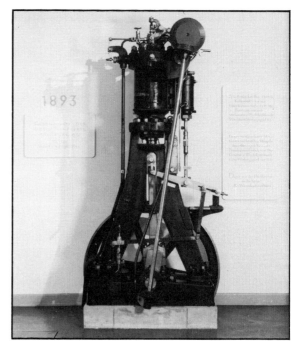

**Above left** A monument in the workshop where huge ship's engines are now made in Augsburg works marks the place where Rudolf Diesel did his research and erected his first engine.

**Above** Diesel's first research engine was built in December 1893 but was not reliable. It was over three years before an effective engine was completed.

**Left** Diesel's first successful engine stands in the Deutsches Museum in Munich and is over 11 feet high excluding the flywheel pit. The cylinder at the right is to power the 'blast-injection' system of introducing fuel to the cylinder.

**Above right** Rudolf Diesel born in 1858 was a talented linguist as well as a brilliant engineer. His single mindedness made him unpopular among German intellectuals and he disappeared from a cross-Channel steamer in 1913 after an unusually vicious attack on his work.

**Above far right** Progression of the company title shows the stages from long wordy names to thankfully short initials.

**Right** Two of Diesel's engines were exhibited in Munich in June 1898 to drive electric generators. They later did this work on a commercial basis, each developing 20 horsepower at 170 rpm.

**Background photograph** Among early diversifications into agriculture was a ploughing and tilling unit built in 1919 with a four-cylinder 45 horsepower petrol engine.

**Inset right** Heaviest of the first range of MAN trucks built at Nürnberg in 1915 was the five ton 45 horsepower model developed from a Saurer design. All heavy models like this had chain drive until the double reduction axle came in 1928.

**Inset below** Lighter chassis in 1915-23 had Cardan shaft drive, in contrast with chains on the heavy models. This is a three tonner chassis, with 36 horsepower engine. Note that even at that early date electric lighting was fitted.

**Left** A contemporary charcoal sketch depicting a Nürnberg street in 1916 shows a typical MAN double-deck bus on a 45 horsepower three tonner chassis. This is a 32 passenger version with MAN's own body.

**Top** Over the first eight years of MAN trucks there was little change in design. Compare this 1923 five tonner with the 1915 model.

**Above** In 1924 petrol engined chassis took the major share of sales. By then a live axle for trucks up to six tons had been perfected, but seven tonners upwards still used chains.

**Right** Heavy trucks in the 1915-22 period were usually fitted with complex wooden wheels, like this one on a 1919 fire engine. The original MAN logo was still used at that time.

# THE DECADES OF DEVELOPMENT

With a busy and profitable commercial vehicle function under way, Anton Rieppel was able to justify an intensification of effort towards the development of the automotive diesel engine that he had for so long anticipated. The fact that truck-sized engines were being built at Nürnberg made things easier, because it became a simple and inexpensive matter to make up special one-off experimental parts in the foundries and machine shops that built the production petrol engines. As the production of the heavy diesel engines for industrial and marine purposes progressed at Augsburg works, a Munich firm of specialist engineers, Friedrich Deckel, became involved in the design and development of fuel injection equipment for those engines. It was natural for Rieppel and his engineers to approach Deckel with their problems in the small diesel engine.

The man responsible for this diesel research at MAN was an engineer called Paul Wiebecke, and from 1916 onwards he worked with Deckel, commuting between Munich, Augsburg and Nürnberg, as the work progressed. For a long time they were torn between the 'blast-injection' system that worked well enough on big engines, and the 'solid-injection' that Ackroyd had used on his pre-chamber engines in England before the turn of the century. The problem was to inject against compression and firing pressures directly into the cylinder without any pressure leakage back through the injector. As early as 1911, direct injection for large-cylinder diesels had been made to work, but scaling that down to a small high-speed engine was extremely difficult with the materials and technology then available. Deckel came up with a solution early in 1921. Why not, he argued, have a non-return valve in the injection pipe to make the whole line go hydraulically 'solid' as soon as there is any reverse flow, instead of trying to make the injector itself do all the work? In 1919 the team built an experimental single cylinder engine using this principle. It proved very difficult to start, but once it

did, it ran surprisingly well and produced ten horsepower at 700 rpm. It was an encouraging turn of events. It had been 22 years since Diesel had got his engine running in a satisfactory manner, and the engineers were getting impatient for an automotive diesel. At last they were getting close.

But there were still many difficulties to overcome. Detonation of the fuel as soon as it was injected led to premature mechanical failure in some test engines. Rough running was another problem and engine structures had to be strengthened considerably to cope with the mechanical stresses. A great deal of detail development about the rate that fuel was injected into the cylinder and the timing of that injection had to be carried out. Finally, in 1923, Wiebecke and Deckel were able to report to a delighted Rieppel that they had overcome all the problems sufficiently to enable them to start work on a proper truck direct injection diesel. The go-ahead was readily granted and by the end of that year the very first direct injection small diesel was completed and run on December 15 1923.

Superficially it looked remarkably like the Saurer-extracted petrol engines used since 1915. It had an aluminium alloy crankcase, with two pairs of cast iron cylinders bolted on. There were detachable cylinder heads, overhead valves operated by external pushrods, and the all-important injection pump mounted low down at the right-hand side of the engine. There were two injectors per cylinder, spraying in horizontally just under the valves. The engine worked admirably, starting problems having been greatly eased by the use of two injectors, and it ran at 900 rpm to develop just 40 horsepower. Its capacity was 6.3 litres, with a bore and stroke of 112 mm by 160 mm. It ran on crude gas oil, and the only problem in starting from cold could be overcome by using a blowlamp on the inlet manifold for a few moments. It was somewhat rough in its running, but not to such an extent that it would be intolerable in a truck. The most important factor was its efficiency which, for the first time in an automotive engine, exceeded 30 per cent; in other words the power it produced was over 30 per cent of the theoretical energy put into it by the fuel. That compared with about 21 per cent in the best petrol engines and nine per cent for steam.

There was considerable jubilation both at Augsburg and Nürnberg where the engine had been jointly built and developed. But there was little time for self congratulation. Over at Mannheim Benz & Comp, together with Rheinische Motorenfabrik, had developed an indirect injection automotive diesel which developed 50 horsepower from a four-cylinder 125 mm by 180 mm engine. The following year was the great International Motor Exhibition in Berlin. The MAN engine was simply a prototype and it needed a lot of detail tidying up and development work before it could be offered as a genuine alternative to the petrol engine. Spurred by the success of their colleagues' programme, the production engineers at Nürnberg got to work on the design and although little was basically changed, the appeareance of the production engine was vastly improved. The two blocks were replaced by a single casting, though two heads were retained. Gone were the untidy and vulnerable external pushrods which now ran in channels through the blocks and heads to rockers enclosed in neat alloy covers. The same basic crankcase design remained and the fuel pump stayed low down on the inlet side of the engine. Detail internal developments led to a power increase to 45 horsepower at 1050 rpm.

When the show opened in Berlin on December 14 1924, the production MAN direct injection diesel truck was there, and the engine made a separate exhibit. Benz also had a diesel truck on show, but this was an indirect injection type, less efficient than the direct injection engine, and it was to be many years before they changed to direct injection. Just as the world's first diesel engine had been developed at MAN, so had the world's first direct injection automotive diesel. They were ready to sell the great economy potential of the diesel to the world.

While the diesel development engineers had been busy producing their new engine, the chassis designers had not been idle. Anticipating the success of the super-economy diesel they had prepared a whole new range of design features intended to make MAN the most modern chassis in Europe. Pneumatic tyres were optional on all chassis except the new seven-ton type by the time the Berlin show opened at the end of 1924, and the engine, clutch and gearbox were all assembled as a single unit instead of being distributed at various points along the chassis as most makers did. The chassis frame was made wider with longer springs directly under

the chassis to reduce the stresses in the structure. Four-wheel brakes were developed on every type.

The diesel power unit's efficiency was very attractive and one of the first substantial orders came from the Bavarian Post Office, who from 1925 onwards built up an extensive fleet of diesel post buses. To enable loading heights for buses to be kept as low as possible, low slung chassis were developed. But possibly the most revolutionary development was a unique axle design that was in principle to remain an MAN trademark for over 40 years. The engineers at Nürnberg who designed and built the truck components had always been less than happy about carrying heavy weights on an axle that also carried the drive through its centre. The stress patterns were incompatible they argued. And although the lighter trucks used the live-axle layout for many years after trucks first emerged from the plant, anything over about five tonnes payload — less in the early days — was fitted with a solid beam axle with chain drive to the wheelhubs from a countershaft on the chassis.

They came up with a clever solution to the problem. A new axle was developed in which the weight was carried by a single solid forged beam, on the ends of which were bolted reduction gear casings that also carried the hubs. A small crownwheel casing was bolted to the centre of the beam, with drive shafts running out to the end casings parallel to the load-carrying main beam. It had several advantages. The gear drive was divided, so parts were smaller and more lightly stressed. Excessive loads could be accommodated without fear of damage to the drive gear. And the axle was easier and cheaper to make than the normal type, at least in heavy capacity classes. From the outset the axle was successful and by the end of 1925 it was fitted to all the new chassis that were coming into production, banishing the chain drive for ever.

Those were momentous years at MAN. Early in 1924 the trucks still looked much the same as the first ones ever made in 1915 — as indeed they might as they were built to the same basic design. The maximum power rating offered was 45 horsepower and the heaviest load capacity was five tonnes. Within two years, ultra modern looking trucks and buses had appeared, with power ratings as high as 150 horsepower. Six-speed gearboxes were offered, and payload capacities of ten and 12 tonnes were introduced at the top of the range. Once over that greatest of hurdles — the successful diesel — all the skill and ingenuity of the designers could be directed towards commercial advancement.

*     *     *

Such was the success of the changes in design that

took place in 1924-26 — not least the diesel engine and the double reduction axle — that enquiries came in from many overseas markets, and MAN set about building an international range of trucks and buses with a proper marketing organisation to handle them. No longer could they simply rely on their goodwill in a limited home market to sell their products, excellent though they were. Those wider geographical horizons in turn meant that the engineering view had to be correspondingly wide, as MAN were freely competing with the world's greatest trucks, from France, Britain, Sweden and the United States.

In many ways the MAN truck building division was fortunate in being part of a very much larger engineering group, the Gutehoffnungshütte or GHH, into which it was absorbed in 1920. That group made big industrial and marine diesel engines, railway stock, printing machinery, bridges and heavy steel structures, power generating plant of all sizes including the world's largest turbines, high pressure boilers, and a wide variety of specialised equipment for industry. From that vast pool of technological experience and skill it was invariably possible to produce the answer to any engineering problem. All it needed was adapting to the scale and economics in question. Consequently as MAN blossomed into a world-class commercial vehicle manufacturer, a significant expansion took place in the facilities at Nürnberg that produced those vehicles.

An illustration of this expansion is that the hall used for assembling all vehicles in 1923-4 was turned over to a service and repair shop in 1925 as a new plant came into use, but that repair shop was inadequate in size by 1930 and had to be expanded. Production that had been limited to less than 20 vehicles a week in 1922-3 expanded to 25-30 a week by 1926, and almost doubled again by 1930. The size of this production necessitated not only a new chassis assembly shop, but new assembly techniques, and towards the end of the 1920s this need was filled by a huge chassis shop at the Nürnberg plant, erected as part of an overall expansion programme instigated by Otto Meyer, who was the works director from the death of Anton Rieppel in 1928 until after the Second World War. Meyer was a big thinker, and his chassis shop was nearly 200 metres long, with rails running full length on which the chassis moved. Chassis were built at right-angles to the length of the shop, cradles under the front axles running on one set, and further cradles under the rear axles running on parallel rails. There were six sets of 'back-end' rails to suit various wheelbases. Opposite the long assembly track, sub-assembly stations were located, so the finished parts were simply wheeled across the aisle to the appropriate place on the track. For its time it was one of the most modern truck plants in Europe and it fed the demand for MANs for many years in a very satisfactory manner. Throughout the 1930s nearly 3000 chassis a year rolled off that line.

But it was not only in chassis assembly that big investment took place. Once the technology of making a successful truck diesel was mastered, an all-out attack was made on the systematic development of high power engines with very low specific fuel consumptions. The first step was a refined version of the 1924 Berlin Show engine, which appeared in mid-1925 in both four- and six-cylinder forms. These were known as respectively the W4V and W6V which developed 45 and 68 horsepower respectively. Not all users were convinced of the diesel's reliability despite its economy and there was still a strong demand for petrol engines, but slowly the diesel made progress. In 1925, 20 W6Vs were built and sold, along with 55 W4Vs, and by 1927 these figures had trebled.

A big step forward was achieved in that year. Instead of the two opposed injectors in the side of each cylinder, a single centre injector type was developed, and that brought about considerable improvements in starting, smoothness and reliability. This injected into a combustion chamber formed in a shallow depression in the cylinder crown and immediately gave a useful step up in power per cylinder. The six-cylinder engine gave 112 horsepower at 1400 rpm, and a special version of this gave 129 horsepower at 1550 rpm, which was probably the fastest revving diesel built anywhere at that date. This engine was installed among other chassis, in an impressively large six wheeler, the S1H type. This was advertised as the most powerful diesel truck in the world. This was undoubtedly true, though it is questionable whether the 150 horsepower claimed for it was genuine, even as a gross figure. The petrol engined version did however have a true 150 horsepower. The truck had a payload capacity of ten tonnes, and could haul a trailer carrying a further three to four tonnes, and was undoubtedly one of the biggest load movers on the roads of Europe at that time. But few hauliers and industrial concerns were very interested in such exotica; their bread and butter was in the three, five and six tonners on two axles, which comprised the bulk of truck production well into the 1930s. But the average size and power of trucks was growing, an inevitable consequence of a nation slowly gathering political and economic dominance in an uneasy continent.

In 1932 a further major development in engine design occurred, with what was called the *Luftkammer* or air chamber type engine. This had a long conical combustion chamber in the cylinder head with a small air chamber leading off it. The idea was that the chamber acted as a sort of shock-absorber for the steep rise of cylinder pressure as combustion took place to reduce the characteristic 'knock' of the diesel. It worked well enough, but MAN's engine designers were still looking for their ideal combustion system. They came much closer to it in 1936 with what was originally called the G-motor (derived from Globus, from the spherical space in the piston crown). By this time Robert Bosch of Stuttgart was supplying the injection equipment and working in close conjunction with the Nürnberg engineers he developed special injectors to suit the new system. The result was a 'revelation in refinement' to quote a contemporary press report. Not only was noise greatly reduced with almost total absence of diesel knock, but higher rotational speeds up to 2400 rpm could be achieved with acceptable smoothness.

## Engine data — 1932-35 Luftkammer types

| | | | |
|---|---|---|---|
| D0534 4 cylinder | 4.57 litre | 47 hp | 105 x 130 mm |
| D0536 6 cylinder | 6.7 litre | 70 hp | 105 x 130 mm |
| D0544 4 cylinder | 4.87 litre | 59 hp | 105 x 140 mm |
| D0546 6 cylinder | 7.3 litre | 88 hp | 105 x 140 mm |
| D2086 6 cylinder | 12.2 litre | 110 hp | 120 x 180 mm |

When you consider the state of the diesel art elsewhere in Europe at that time, the MAN engines stand out as advanced specimens indeed. Most of the other popular diesels were still pre-chamber indirect injection types, including both Leyland and AEC, while Daimler Benz were only just beginning direct injection experiments in search of higher efficiency. Gardner engines had direct injection, but were slower revving than most, while many manufacturers used Saurer patents, all of which were indirect injection types. The powerful MAN types made superb passenger vehicle engines, and MANs were at the time the most sought after coach chassis. Some very elaborate bodywork examples were built on their fast, quiet chassis. The typical German coach of the period was a big, square, aggressive looking machine championed by Büssing, but a fashion in streamlined elegant designs with distinctly French styling grew up around the MANs. Meanwhile in the truck world, MAN had to discontinue the presentation of bronze, silver and gold medals to truck owners whose vehicles had done 100,000, 200,000 or 300,000 kilometres because of the number of claimants.

Throughout this 1930s period the emphasis was on evolution rather than revolution in design. Once the direct injection diesel and MAN's distinctive double reduction axle had been established as keystones in the overall design, the development of chassis progressed as a series of detail improvements over a period of about 13 years, rather than with spectacular new designs appearing periodically. Frames became stiffer with the addition of cruciform bracing and suspension became more comfortable with longer springs and hydraulic damping. But the majority of trucks remained as bonneted two-axle types with a sprinkling of six wheelers, although a gradual evolution of styling took place, with radiators becoming raked back instead of upright and cabs taking on a more rounded less severe outline. An illustration of the supremacy of the MAN designs came from a big international diesel truck rally which was run from Moscow to Tiflis and back in Russia towards the end of 1934. The total distance was well over 5000 kilometres and altitudes over 7000 feet were reached crossing the Caucasus mountains on the southern part of the trek. The four MAN entries were among ten direct injection types, competing against 13 indirect injection models, and seven semi-diesels including Hesselman conversions of Volvos from Sweden and a dozen Russian trucks. Three of the MANs ran the whole distance without stoppage, among only seven in the entire entry that did so. In the cold-starting trials up in the mountains, the MANs recorded an average of nine seconds against 12 seconds average for the direct injection entries, and 33 seconds average for the indirect class. The 90 horsepower D0546-engined MAN was the outright winner, with two other MANs in the first five, including a 110 horsepower 12.2 litre D2086 in third place.

This success was widely reported in both trade and general press reports, and made the MAN reputation even more famous. At the next Berlin Show, in 1936, the company's exhibits included two of the successful Russian-trip types, together with the new G-motor, fitted in a luxury touring coach and a mobile radio studio. There was also a chassis running on petroleum gas as an experimental project. All chassis by that date had a radiator mascot in the form of a ring with the MAN logo across it, rather like the shape of the modern Martini logo.

## MAN Model range — 1937

| Type | Payload (tonnes) | Gross weight (tonnes) | Engine | Power |
|---|---|---|---|---|
| E2 | 2.5/3 | 6.5 | 4 cyl 4.5 litre | 65 hp |
| D1 | 4/4.5 | 8.0 | 6 cyl 6.7 litre | 75 hp |
| Z1 & Z2 | 6 | 10 | 6 cyl 7.3 litre | 90 hp |
| M1 | 7/7.5 | 12 | 6 cyl 8.4 litre | 100 hp |
| F1/F2 | 8 | 14 | 6 cyl 8.4 litre | 110 hp |
| F4 | 8/8.5 | 15 | 8 cyl 12 litre | 150 hp |

Bus variants were offered on E2, Z1 and M1 chassis.

**Above far left** Truck-sized direct injection engine technology achieved a breakthrough in 1919 when this single cylinder test engine ran successfully. It turned out ten horsepower at 700 rpm. Deckel's experimental 'air-less' pump is seen on the left.

**Above left** The prototype automotive diesel engine did not appear until 1923 — a quarter of a century after Rudolf Diesel made his engine work. This engine is now in the Deutsches Museum, and its resemblance to the original Saurer pattern petrol engine is apparent.

**Above** When the prototype diesel was installed in a well-worn works truck, experimental equipment was still attached. Pipes to transfer excess fuel to the inlet ports are visible, and the truck's original petrol engine is still on the body at the back.

**Left** The first bus to have the new diesel engine in 1924 was also a well-used example, but it was not long before new buses were being so fitted.

**Right** The first production truck diesels were much cleaner and more refined than the prototype and developed 45 horsepower at 1050 rpm. Note that each injector pipe divides to feed a sprayer on each side of the head.

**Above** The 1925 catalogue used a picture of a heavily laden brewer's dray with the W4V diesel engine inset to advertise the working ability of their new development. Note the chain controls to the engine.

**Right** The speedy advance of bus design is illustrated by a contemporary sketch of the production shop in 1923, a mere eight years after the first buses were made. **Inset** Very low profiles were a MAN feature in the mid-1920s.

**Below** Production W4V four-cylinder diesel engine in unit with clutch and gearbox was a star exhibit at the International Motor Show in Berlin in December 1924.

**Above** This rather heavily retouched photograph of the MAN stand at the 1924 Berlin Show was widely published in the press. The exciting new diesel engine can be seen in the centre in front of a diesel truck.

**Left** A new model, the NOG-4 was shown in prototype at the 1924 Berlin Show although it did not go into full production until the following year. Its appearance was very similar to that of the Leyland Lioness of the 1928-31 period. This is the production 1926 version.

**Top right** Ultra low build was a feature of MAN buses throughout the 1920s. This 26 seater town bus was built in 1926.

**Right** The 1928 seven ton diesel chassis was fitted with the W4V four-cylinder engine with the W6V six-cylinder as an option. Although the chassis was quite advanced solid tyres were still used. But by the end of that year the petrol engined version (**centre right**) had pneumatic tyres.

**Left** The Nürnberg production line in 1932 was capable of turning out nearly 3,000 chassis a year. Chassis were moved on rail-borne trollies until they were self mobile.

**Top** In 1927 MAN built an impressive ten tonne payload six wheeler, billed as the world's most powerful diesel truck. That was undoubtedly true though it is doubtful if it had 150 genuine horsepower at that time.

**Above** An elaborately styled coach on a 1935 chassis typifies many efforts of that period. In this case the grille follows the pattern of the BMW motor cars.

**Right** Since 1928 MAN have always had double reduction axles. Most of them were of this type where load-carrying and drive members were quite separate.

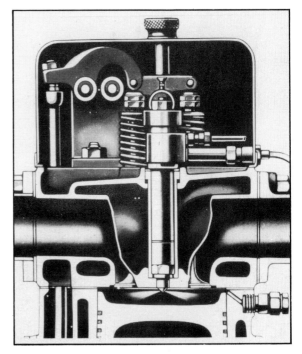

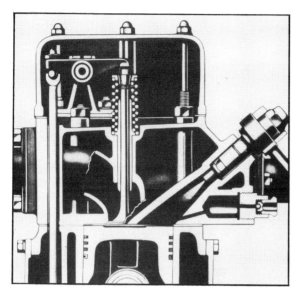

The drawings on these pages show five stages in the development of MAN's direct injection diesels: (**far left**) 1924 — two opposed injectors; (**left**) 1927 — central injection; (**above**) 1932 — *Luftkammer* type; (**right**) 1936 — G-motor; (**below right**) 1940 — M-system engine.

**Far left** The diesel took a big upward step in efficiency with the *Luftkammer* engine in 1933. It was this design which brought success in the 1934 Russian diesel rally.

**Left and below** The first engine with the spherical combustion chamber was the 1936 G-motor, like this sectioned example.

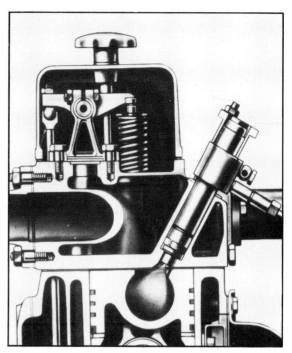

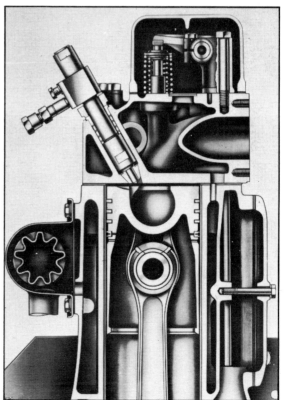

**This page** MAN trucks in the 1930s were all four-wheeled bonnetted types, and sloping radiators began to appear around 1934. Despite the unchanging external style, considerable mechanical refinement took place.

**Above right** Powerful tractors were produced at Nürnberg in the 1930s. This 1938 version had a 50 horsepower diesel and power-tilling gear.

**Right** Type F4 chassis in 1936-40 had an inline eight-cylinder 150 horsepower and ran at 15 tonnes gross, or 25 tonnes with a trailer.

# THE ASCENT OF MAN

As the war approached, a large part of the entire MAN manufacturing facility was turned over to making military equipment, and that included most of the vehicle plant at Nürnberg. The engines with the spherical combustion chamber — now called the M-system — had been so successful that they had ousted the petrol engine from trucks entirely by 1939. Diesels were built for a wide variety of military applications, including tanks and submarines, and the plant worked day and night turning out military trucks and a limited number for civilian use too. The majority of civil truck production was concentrated round the little three tonne E2 model, a four-cylinder 65 horsepower bonneted truck that first emerged in 1936 at the Berlin show, and it was on the backs of these tough little four wheelers that German commerce continued during the period of hostilities. All the heavier chassis were adopted for military use in one form or another and no actual new designs appeared after 1938.

During the latter stages of the war, the Nürnberg plant was extensively damaged by bombing, and the truck assembly plant completely destroyed. So was much of the Augsburg works, and major reconstruction was called for before serious production could begin again. All that remained in effect, was the skill of the men who had built MAN trucks before the war. But it was not only the truck plant that was gone. Practically the whole of the giant group was affected and the heavy industrial engineering works had to take priority. But late in 1946, in a small corner of the temporary building on what had been the Nürnberg works site, work began on a new truck. The design originated from 1939 but had never been translated into metal. It was a classically simple machine, a four wheeler with weight capacity from five to eight tonnes payload, and room for either a four- or six-cylinder engine, depending on the length of the front chassis overhang. This was the famous model MK, perhaps the toughest and most versatile truck that MAN ever built. That characteristic

could not have emerged at a more opportune time.

The reconstruction of a war-ravaged nation depended heavily on the number of trucks available to fetch and carry, haul and heave everything from badly needed foodstuffs to new building materials. For a long time MAN's contribution was limited to as many chassis as could be hand-built in the corner of the works, and until the middle of 1947 that only amounted to a handful. But finally the truck plant got its turn in the order of priority and before 1947 was out, a steady flow of about 20 chassis a week was emerging. There were two basic models, the MK25 which was a solo truck for general duties with a 120 horsepower six-cylinder diesel, and the MK26 which was a heavier duty chassis for construction work or for trailer hauling with a 132 horsepower diesel. A few four-cylinder types were made too. All of course had the familiar double reduction axle, and gearboxes were supplied by the Zahnradfabrik Friedrichshafen, known widely as ZF.

These models formed the basis of the truck range for the next eight years, although there were many variants. There was, for example, a V8 engined 180 horsepower truck called the F8 built mainly as a tractor with a 19 tonne train weight, though some 16 tonne six wheelers were built too. That emerged in 1952, when the German economy was beginning to get into its stride again, and the thoughts of industrialists were once again turning to big capacity high speed transport. Equally important were the passenger versions of the MK, known as the MKN type with a bonneted layout, and the MKP with forward control. Both used the same M-system six-cylinder diesel engine with 120 horsepower, driving through a ZF five-speed gearbox. The ultimate development in the MK series was the MKH, a rear engined version built for both urban and intercity work, and believed to be one of the first successful rear-engined buses to emerge after the war. That was in 1950, and the following year the MKE electric trolley bus was produced to augment the severely overloaded public transport systems in many German cities.

All this activity severely strained the resources of the small plant at Nürnberg, which was concentrating on large turbines, railway machinery and heavy electrical gear at the time. There was an urgent need for more capacity, for although by 1954 output had reached the prewar level, demand was far in excess of that figure. The solution was not long in appearing. Just to the north-west of Munich was a huge factory that had turned out BMW aircraft engines during the war and somehow emerged undamaged. It was used by the American forces as a base repair workshop for some years but came up for disposal in 1955. It was a vast site, some 692,000 square metres (171 acres) of which about a quarter was occupied by sound factory buildings. It was close to a railway line and just a few kilometres outside the big city of Munich itself. It was an ideal place to build trucks. With the site went a genuine mediaeval castle, somewhat battered and neglected at that date, but part of the contract with the Public Works Office was that the castle should be restored and maintained by MAN, and it stands to this day in a small wood just behind the plant. Otto Meyer was still works director in charge of road vehicles and his had been the burden of struggling with inadequate space and materials throughout the reconstruction period. He planned the Munich works on highly rationalised lines to produce a series of basic components that could be used in all kinds of trucks, farm tractors, buses and coaches, simply by making detailed changes. Meyer's vision in so doing was a major factor in ensuring the survival of MAN vehicles in the severely competitive world that was to follow in the 1960s and 1970s.

All vehicle production was switched to Munich from mid-1955, and the first farm tractor was completed on September 6, followed by the first truck on November 15. Engine production remained at Nürnberg, where there were foundries and heavy machining shops, but all other production moved to Munich. Just as production began in the new plant, the main board decided to give the vehicle division of MAN the status of a separate company within the group, instead of merely a division of the light engineering company. MAN Nutzfahrzeuge was its name and soon after it was formed Otto Meyer, who had spent much of his life working towards that goal, finally retired.

\*  \*  \*  2034975

The very first trucks to emerge from the new Munich plant were still based on the old warhorse MK type, which had an enviable reputation not only in Germany itself but in an increasing number of overseas markets, notably South America. But despite its extreme reliability and toughness, it was decidedly old fashioned, did not lend itself particularly well to volume production, and a new model range was needed. The new technical director was Dr Kurt Kries and he led his engineering teams in a total redesign of the entire road vehicle range. Engine designs continued to use the steadily developing M-system, which in turn was a direct descendant of the prewar G-motor. M stood for *Mittelkugel* or central-sphere, which was a description of the combustion chamber. All MAN automotive engines since that date have used the same basic system which has a coil-shaped inlet port which lines up with the contours of the spherical combustion chamber to produce a high-speed rotational movement to the combustion gases both before and after ignition. A range of rationalised chassis was drawn up, mostly of bonneted layout, but providing a longer than average loadspace in relation to the wheelbase by virtue of a set-back front axle. A stylish cab design was evolved with a distinct appearance common to all types. The new truck range comprised seven basic models, although there were some variations for special applications.

Although these trucks may seem to overlap somewhat in their specification and ability they were in fact built for quite distinct applications. Suspension, transmission and tyre specifications drew clear distinctions between those models for express highway use and those for heavy duty work like construction or timber haulage.

The engine numbering system used in that range

## MAN 1955 truck range

| Chassis | Gross vehicle weight | Gross train weight | Engine type | Power output | Top speed |
|---|---|---|---|---|---|
| 515.L1 | 10,800 kg | 26,800 kg | 6 cyl D1046 7983 cc | 115 bhp @ 2100 rpm | 67 kph |
| 630L2 | 12,900 kg | 36,900 kg | 6 cyl D1246 8276 cc | 135 bhp @ 2100 rpm | 69 kph |
| 630L2a | 13,500 kg | 37,500 kg | 6 cyl D1246 8276 cc | 135 bhp @ 2100 rpm | 67 kph |
| 758L1 | 15,000 kg | 39,000 kg | 8 cyl D1048 10644 cc | 155 bhp @ 2000 rpm | 70 kph |
| 750TL1 | 15,000 kg | 39,000 kg | 6 cyl D1246T 8276 cc (Turbocharged) | 156 bhp @ 2000 rpm | 71 kph |
| 830L2 | 15,000 kg | 37,000 kg | 6 cyl D1246 8276 cc | 135 bhp @ 2100 rpm | 71 kph |
| F8 | 16,000 kg | 40,000 kg | V8 cyl D1548 11633 cc | 180 bhp @ 2000 rpm | 62 kph |

has been continued ever since and the 'code' enables a great deal to be learned about an individual engine. The D stands for diesel, of course, and the first two numbers represent the cylinder bore minus 100 in millimetres. Thus a D10-engine has 110 mm bore, and a D15 — a 115 mm bore. The next digit is rather less than a precise description but it represents the approximate stroke measurement. So a D104 — has a stroke of 140 mm, and a D255 — has a stroke of 150 mm approximately. It will be seen that all the 1955 range of engines were rationalised at 140 mm stroke. The last digit represents the number of cylinders, so the D1046 is a six-cylinder engine and the D1548 is an eight-cylinder type. Most engines have a letter M added to their number, for M-system combustion, and if there is a T, that means it is turbocharged. It will be seen that there was a turbocharged production engine in the 1955 line-up and although MAN made a number of 'blown' engines before that, that particular truck, the 750TL1, was their first turbocharged catalogued model. The turbocharger was a much more complex device than today's designs, with pre-loaded conical bearings, but it worked tolerably well and boosted the output of the 8¼ litre D1246 engine from 135 to 156 horsepower. All these engines were remarkably economical, with specific fuel consumption around 155 grams/horsepower/hour, which in Imperial measure is 0.35 pounds/horsepower/hour, a very good figure indeed by any standards.

This model range was an instant success and by 1959 over 10,000 chassis a year were leaving the works. But already the market demands, particularly overseas, dictated further updating and the first stage towards this was a completely new cab design. The initial drawings began soon after the Munich factory got into full swing in the mid-1950s and over the next three years, styling models gave way to prototypes. Then press tools were made and in 1960 a handsome new range emerged, with both bonneted and full forward control versions, both looking remarkably alike as regards overall styling. The presswork was done at a new plant within the Munich factory. Curved windscreens were incorporated for the first time, and a sleeper cab version was offered for both the bonnetted and forward control models. The chassis line-up was much as before except that the old F8 V8 engine model was dropped and a turbocharged version of the D12 engine introduced with 180 horsepower instead.

The new-look MANs were an enormous success, and large numbers began to go to markets like South America and Africa as well as Europe. By the end of 1961 a factory reorganisation was needed and a new assembly track, nearly 300 metres long, was installed. This enabled production to be increased considerably and by the end of 1962 a rate of 12,000 chassis a year was reached. At that time, a further step in the engine programme was taken, and a developed version of the existing engine range put into production after several years of proving trials. This was the D21 engine introduced in 1963, a range of power units all rationalised around a 121 mm bore and produced in four-cylinder, six-cylinder and turbocharged versions. These were known as the HM engines, a higher efficiency version of the M-system models, achieved by detail development of injection and combustion characteristics. The engines were, of course, still produced at Nürnberg as they are today.

With that range a new chassis numbering system was instigated, comprising two groups of numbers. The first group signified the gross vehicle weight of the chassis, and the second the power output of the engine. These were approximate only, but it was a sensible system, retained to this day. So a 15.210 was a 15 tonne gross vehicle weight chassis with a 210 horsepower engine. The tonnage figure could be misleading, especially in the case of tractive units, where a 15 tonne gross vehicle weight chassis might run at 36 or 38 tonnes gross train weight.

Despite the success of that range of trucks, economic pressures loomed large on the horizons of the 1960s, demanding drastic action if MAN was to survive as a major truck builder. The forward control cab was not spacious enough for many world markets, and a new cab was needed, although the bonneted type was more than adequate for construction trucks and similar types. So an agreement was entered into with Saviem, effective from 1969, whereby MAN would buy pressings from Saviem's pressed steel plant at Blainville in Normandy and assemble them into forward control cabs at Munich. In return, Saviem were to obtain their engines for heavier trucks from MAN at Nürnberg and these comprised most of the D21 range, plus a new 15 litre V8 engine that MAN had developed to meet the new 8 bhp per tonne requirement in Germany and certain other markets. That engine is still used in the Saviem 340 but was only used by MAN for four years in the 19.304 chassis. The bonneted cab was modified with the whole front end lifting up to display the engine, instead of having a hatch-type of access in the top as before. The light truck range was changed to what was in effect a total Saviem design with MAN badges, while in France Saviem sold MAN tippers and construction trucks with simply the name badge changed to Saviem. It was an unusual agreement, but it worked well in almost every facet and much of it is retained into the late-1970s, particularly the cab and engine supply arrangements.

Another unique agreement, entered into towards the end of the 1960s, was with Daimler Benz. The two companies agreed to co-operate on the design and production of major components, notably engines and drive axles, and the first production units began to appear in 1970. Briefly, a rationalised engine range with both vee and inline cylinder versions were jointly developed, MAN to use mainly the inlines and Mercedes the vees, although both partners 'overlapped' into the other's sector to some extent. Major parts like cylinder blocks, cranks, connecting rods and timing gears (which are at the back of the engines next to the flywheel) are common to both makers, while pistons, cylinder heads and detail hardware are individual. The idea was to increase the volume of production of major expensive parts to the point where unit costs could be kept low and this was achieved successfully in practice. The axle programme was similarly orientated and a very tough hub reduction design was evolved, with several weight capacities, numerous ratios, and rear or front-end applications, with variations for single or tandem drive installations. But the basic expensive components were all rationalised to keep the costs relatively low. These axles were immensely successful and are now used on all MAN and Mercedes heavy trucks including military types and earth movers.

A steady programme of refinement was applied to the MAN vehicles, and they came to be known as the quietest most comfortable trucks in Europe. All the time the 8 bhp per tonne rule applied in Germany the big V10 D2530 320 horsepower engine was fitted in the top-of-the-range 16-320 38 tonners, but when that rule was finally dropped in 1976 no time was lost in introducing a new model, the 16/19-280. This used a turbocharged version of the inline six-cylinder engine, the D2566MTF, which had a longer stroke at 155 mm than the majority of the D25 series, and with special pistons and manifolds became one of the most economical engines in Europe. Its success was phenomenal and within a year of its introduction it was occupying nearly half of MAN's domestic market sales of all classes, was approaching 25 per cent of all their European sales, and won the International Truck of the Year Award for 1977-78.

In the meantime, highly mobile military vehicles were developed initially for the Bundeswehr, but later for civilian cross-country applications too. These types introduced a new approach to chassis and suspension design, and had a highly spectacular cross-country performance, all the more remarkable because it was achieved using basically standard engines and axles, without the complexities of

## Basic MAN truck range for mid-1970s

a = truck, b = tractive unit, c = tipper, d = all-wheel drive, *italics* = underfloor engine

| Model No | Chassis layout | Engine/ hp | Gross weight vehicle/combination tonnes | Models |
|---|---|---|---|---|
| 6.115 | 4x2 | D21/115 | 7.5/11 | a b c |
| 11.136 | 4x2 | D21/136 | 11.0/17 | a c |
| 13.168 | 4x2 | D21/168 | 13.0/19 | a b c |
| 13.192 | 4x2 | D25/192 | 13.0/19 | *a* |
| 15/16.168 | 4x2 and 4x4 | D21/168 | 16/32 | a b c d |
| 15/16.200 | 4x2 and 4x4 | D25/200 | 16/32 | a b c d |
| 15/16.240 | 4x2 and 4x4 | D25/240 | 16/32 | a b c d |
| 19.220 | 4x2 and 4x4 | D25/220 | 19/38 | a b c d |
| 19.240 | 4x2 and 4x4 | D25/240 | 19/38 | a b c d |
| 19.280 | 4x2 and 4x4 | D25/280 | 19/40 | a b c d |
| 19.320 | 4x2 and 4x4 | D25/320 | 19/44 | *a* b c d |
| 20.185 | 6x4 | D21/168 | 20/24 | a c |
| 22.240 | 6x2 and 6x4 | D25/240 | 22/32 | *a* |
| 22.280 | 6x2 and 6x4 | D25/280 | 22/34 | a c |
| 22.320 | 6x2 | D25/320 | 22/38 | b |
| 26.240 | 6x4 and 6x6 | D25/240 | 26/36 | a b c d |
| 26.280 | 6x4 and 6x6 | D25/280 | 26/40 | a b c d |
| 26.320 | 6x4 and 6x6 | D25/320 | 26/44 | a b c d |
| 30.280 | 6x4 and 6x6 | D25/280 | 30/60 | a b d |
| 30.320 | 6x4 and 6x6 | D25/320 | 30/80 | a b d |
| 32.320 | 6x6 | D25/320 | 32/100 | b d |

**Note**: This is the basic range only, excluding many variations.

independent suspension and the like so often found on specialist vehicles. In the late 1970s, production reached almost 20,000 chassis a year, of which 2600 were buses. This was a noteworthy performance in view of the fact that the serious economic recessions of the early 1970s had reduced total production in 1973 to a mere 13,000, which was little more than it had been in the early 1960s when the Munich plant had begun their new truck range. The main reason for that fall was the almost total collapse of the construction truck markets in Europe due to legislative controls on public building, and that was MAN's strongest field at the time.

But the bus side of MAN's activity saw a steady growth throughout the late 1960s and 1970s. It took a long time following the opening of the Munich plant to get a modern bus production programme under way, but new underfloor and rear-engined types were launched in 1959 and by 1961 a steady flow of buses to the new designs were available. Up until then all the buses had been based on the old MK series, and were very outdated indeed. The new models were unique in their use of air suspension, noise insulation, stiff safety-conscious structures,

and of course the efficient M-system engines. The majority were rear-engined, as were almost all continental buses and coaches by that time. By the time the late 1960s came, MAN was a major bus supplier in Germany, and was invited to take part in the VöV experiment to produce a rationalised bus for a large number of German city authorities, sharing the scheme with Mercedes Benz, Büssing and Magirus Deutz. The VöV scheme (Verband öffentlicher Verkersbetriebe, or Federation of Public Transport Authorities) was successful, and MAN are to this day building large numbers of city buses to the rationalised pattern set down by the Verband. But the touring coach business was picking up too, as was the demand for urban express coaches, and in 1965 it was decided to make bus production a separate operation, as the large volume of detail work in bus assembly processes was incompatible with that of trucks. A new plant was opened at Penzburg, about 50 kilometres to the south of Munich in 1967, and from then on the bus and coach division operated as a separate entity, and very successfully too. Later on the Büssing bus facility at Watenstedt was added to the group.

**Below** By 1945 and the end of the Second World War the factories were useless heaps of rubble. From this, truck production emerged within a few short months at Nürnberg, though it was to be several years before full production resumed.

**Right** First postwar chassis was the MK series. Its durability was legendary and made a big contribution to the economic rebuilding of Germany in the 1946-54 period.

Typ **F8**

**M·A·N**
**SCHWERST-LASTWAGEN**

mit 8-Zylinder-Diesel-M-Motor in V-Anordnung
bei 180 PS Leistung und einem Gesamtgewicht
von 16 to im Inland und 22 to im Ausland

**Above** Page from the 1949 MAN catalogue shows various types of application for the top-of-the-range F8 model, with the 180 horsepower V8 engine. The F8 came in weight capacities from 16 to 22 tonnes.

**Left** The first truck off the new line at Munich in November 1955 was a 515.L1, and a short ceremony marked the occasion.

Trucks from the new Munich plant in 1955 were sturdy bonnetted types with ancestry in the legendary MK type of 1946. They were (**right**) the 10.8 tonne 115 horsepower 515.L1; (**above right**) the 12.9 tonne 135 horsepower 630.L2; (**overleaf above**) the 13.5 tonne 630.L2a; and top of the line, (**overleaf below**) the 758.L1 a 15 tonne 155 horsepower eight cylinder-type. Others were added in 1956 to make a seven model line-up.

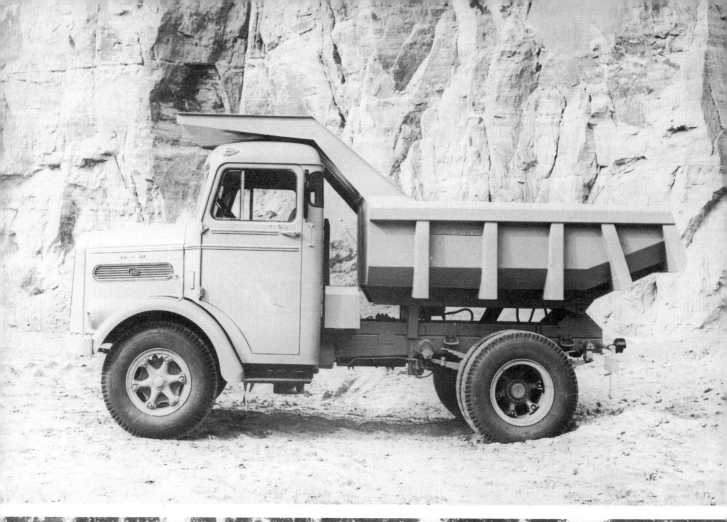

**Above** The Munich truck factory started production in 1955. This view was photographed in 1970. The vacant space near the test track (top left) is now occupied by new research and development workshops.

**Right** MAN's first volume production forward control truck was the MKF series built from 1953 onwards. At that time coachbuilt cabs were still used.

**Left** In 1954, just before truck production moved to Munich, the Nürnberg engine factory began making this D1246 six-cylinder MH-type diesel for heavy trucks. It developed 130 horsepower at 2,000 rpm.

**Right** The 750TL1 was the first production turbocharged truck from the MAN plant, produced from 1956 on. This catalogue extract shows how the turbocharger was arranged on the six-cylinder 155 horsepower engine.

**Below** The integral-structure MKH2 rear-engined bus broke new ground in MAN's bus development programme. It had a 130 horsepower D1246 diesel rear-mounted in unit with a ZF gearbox, driving forwards to the double reduction axle.

**This page** Styling sketches for a new cab began in 1956 which were translated into production pressings in 1960. But as early as 1957 a clay and wood model showed the shape of things to come.

**Left** Engine production for MAN diesels has always been at Nürnberg. This picture was taken in 1954.

This page The new pressed-steel cab of 1960 was a handsome design. The following year a forward control version was introduced, and between them these trucks sold worldwide.

Right Demand for the new pressed steel cab necessitated new press, assembly and paint shops at Munich, which came into full production in 1961.

**Above left** A 40 horsepower diesel tractor of the type that was first built at Munich in 1955, working on a forestry site with power winches front and back.

**Left, and the following six pages** The steel-cab forward and normal control MAN range in the 1960s succeeded in virtually every role of road transport, both in Germany and in export markets.

**Above** With the model update of 1969 three distinct cabs were used. Forward control cabs (left) were assembled from pressings imported from France, while construction industry trucks (right) used the short bonnetted style introduced at Munich in 1960. Light trucks (centre) were SG-series Saviems slightly modified to suit German regulations.

**Right** Tilt-cab models were introduced in 1969 using a new cab structure built from pressings supplied by Saviem. Sleeper cab versions were added a little later. This cab remains in use today.

**Left** Full lift-up front ends were introduced on the normal control trucks in 1971, instead of the hatch-type engine access. The radiator from that time on was mounted to the engine, not to the chassis.

**Below** The introduction of the spacious Saviem-origin cab made MANs very popular all over Europe. This timber haulier is disembarking from the Bodensee ferry in 1970.

**Right** On the Munich production line chassis begin in an inverted position while axles and springs are added. They are turned over for the addition of engines and superstructure.

**Below right** Chassis undergoing final test and check in a special hall at the end of the Munich assembly track. The insulation under the cab floor is clearly visible on the tilted cab.

## MAN

**Left** A 26.256 6x4 mixer chassis works on the construction of the Olympic Stadium in Munich early in 1972. This version used the D 2538 V8 engine.

**Below** Standard city buses to VöV specifications worked at the 1972 Olympics transporting athletes and officials between stadiums and living quarters.

**Right** Operators all over Europe use MANs as the mainstay of their long-haul fleets like this big fleet user in Linz, Austria, who runs regular freight services throughout the EEC.

**Below right** Ride and handling qualities on the modern MANs enable them to tackle tricky situations like this with a high degree of safety.

**Background photograph** One of the heaviest ever tasks for MANs was the building of a new airport at Nice. More than 60 24.320 6x6 tractive units hauling 100 tons of earth and rock per trip moved 30 million tons a distance of 12 kilometres, moving a whole mountain into the sea in 1976-77. The side-tipping trailers had retarders fitted.

**Left inset** The MAN 16.232 was introduced to Britain after the 1972 Commercial Vehicle Show. It uses the D2556 engine with 12 speed ZF gearbox, and was joined by the 16-280 turbocharged version in 1976.

**Right inset** A special UK-market 30 ton rigid eight wheeler was developed in 1974. It was called the 30.232 VF and used identical mechanical units to the 32 ton tractive units.

**Above left** A heavy haulage version of the 38-330 fitted with the ZF WSK-type transmission was developed in 1975. This UK-registered but left-hand drive example is recovering a derelict German tank from Jack Hardwick's yard at Ewell.

**Left** One of the most successful modern MANs is the normal control 26-240 6x4 tipper. Although rated at 26 tonnes gross on-highway most examples can be found carrying well over 20 tonnes payload on construction sites. This one is working on a new road in Luxemburg.

**Above** Heaviest of the MAN tipper range is the 38-320 6x6 dumper, fitted at the factory with Meiller dumper body. All three axles use the same hub reduction layout.

**Right** A production special-cab version of the 19-280 and 19-320 trucks included special food storage and cooking arrangements for use on long intercontinental hauls.

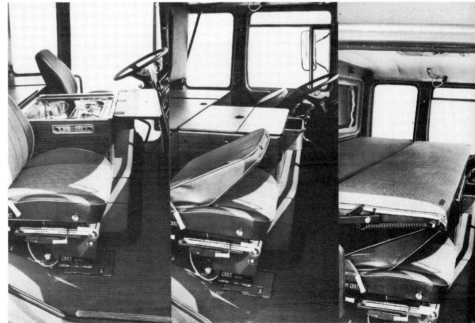

**Left and below far left** The earlier tilt-cab highway trucks had a steering column mounted gear-shift, but this was moved to the floor in 1977 because of higher shift-loads in syncromesh gearboxes.

**Below left and bottom left** Extremes of suspension design on the same rationalised axle are the very stiff dump truck leaf springs with 22 plates, and the ultra-soft and smooth air suspension on the 1977 19-280 tractive unit.

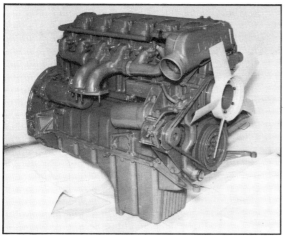

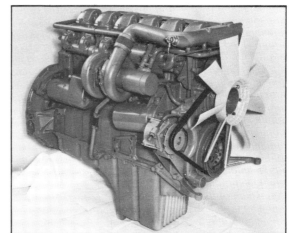

Three principal truck engines in the D25 range are (**above**) the D2556 230 horsepower; (**above right**) the D2566MTF turbocharged 280-290 horsepower unit, and (**top**) the D2530 V10 320-330 horsepower unit that powers the top weight trucks.

**Right** Downturned axle end on the 26-240 and 26-280 tippers increases ground clearance without resort to special springs.

**Above** The D2530 V10 320 horsepower engine fits very snugly in the 19-320 chassis. Note the exhaust brake valve on the end of the manifold.

**Below** Many special versions of the D25 engines are built. This is a 460 horsepower V10 with twin turbochargers, built for use in railcars. It uses water charge cooling to control induction-air temperatures.

**Right** D25 pistons have iron inserts for the top ring and the rim of the spherical combustion chamber. On turbocharged engines there is an annular oil cooling channel under the crown.

**Far right** Section of the D2566MTF engine shows the simple layout, and details like the piston crown oil channel, spherical combustion chamber, iron piston inserts and the wet liners.

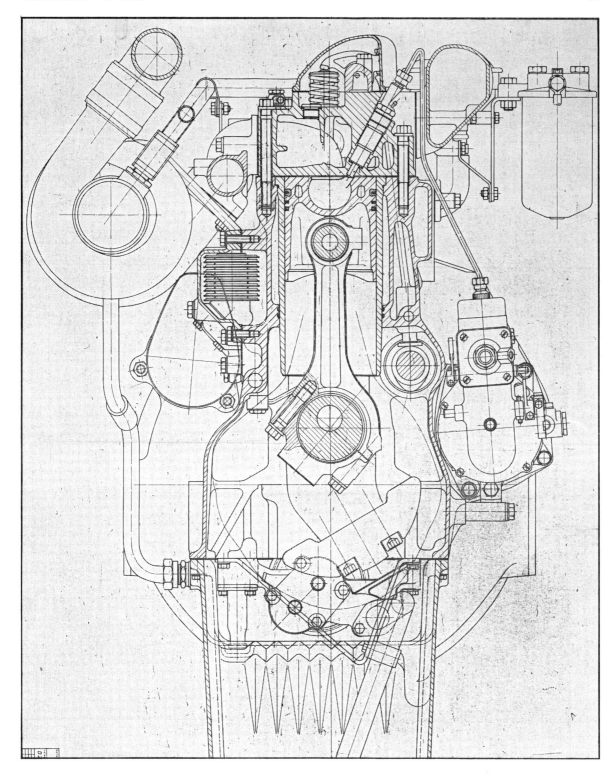

# NEW NAMES, NEW IDEAS, NEW MARKETS

Perhaps more than any other European manufacturer, MAN has extensive and sometimes complicated relationships with manufacturers in other countries outside Germany. The agreements with Saviem in France and Daimler Benz have already been described, but those are just two of many. In Austria for example, the Österreichische Automobilfabrik, or ÖAF company has for many years been a wholly owned MAN subsidiary. They are in Vienna, and now also own the very old Viennese Gräf und Stift company which makes buses. That subsidiary is known by the cumbersome title of Österreichische Automobilfabrik und Gräf Und Stift AG, but the trucks are known as ÖAFs and the buses by the Gräf und Stift badge. Trucks and buses are both built under licence from MAN, although the Austrian factories produce their own designs for special purposes as well. D25 series rationalised engines are purchased from Nürnberg for the majority of power requirements in the Viennese products.

In Rumania, the Roman group builds trucks under direct licence from MAN. These have a locally pressed and assembled version of the modern Saviem cab, and the old D21 series engines, with imported ZF gearboxes. The Romans are more like Saviems than modern MANs in fact, but sell well in many markets. The engines were originally bought from Raba in Hungary, but Roman now have their own engine plant. The Hungarian Raba operation is based round a large foundry and machining plant which turns out MAN-licensed D21 engines, both for its own use and for supplying to other users in the geographical region, including a number of industrial engine applications. Unlike Roman, Raba imports the complete cab from MAN and the ZF transmissions are imported too. The Ikarus bus factory is also in Hungary but apart from being powered by the MAN-licensed D21 Raba engine, there is no direct connection with MAN itself despite some styling similarities. Down in Yugoslavia,

Automontagge Ljubljana make very tough rugged buses, suitable for the less-than-perfect roads that exist in the majority of that country. These were originally MAN domestic designs, but were modified with extra ground clearance, stiffened considerably to accept the rough use, and are highly successful buses. Engines are purchased direct from Nürnberg. A few trucks are turned out there too, but the majority of production is taken up by buses.

There are a number of licencees further afield. In India, for example, ShaktiMAN (strong-MAN, locally translated) builds a range of the more rugged MAN designs for local consumption and for military use, while there is an assembly plant in Gabon. Wholly owned subsidiaries exist for local assembly and import in South Africa, Turkey, Australia, Pakistan, Indonesia and the Philippines. Consequently the influence of MAN technology is extensive.

At home there is a new joint enterprise with Volkswagen to produce a range of light and medium trucks between the 4.2 tonne VW LT and the lower end of the MAN medium truck range, which means trucks from four to 14 tonnes. Cabs will be based on the VW LT pressings, but on a stronger subframe enabling the cab to tilt. Engines are being built to a new pattern, the D02 series, and versions are to be made with four or six cylinders developing 90 horsepower and 136 horsepower respectively, plus a turbocharged 179 horsepower type. This range will be built in considerable numbers—sales of over 12,000 a year shared between the two companies are being forecast—and will represent a big challenge to the existing makes in the field, particularly Iveco, Ford, Bedford and the Club of Four (Saviem, Daf, Magirus, Volvo).

In 1971 the whole equity of the old-established Büssing Automobilwerk AG, based in Brunswick was bought by MAN, and Büssing sadly ceased to exist as a separate entity. However, a great deal of the company's know-how lived on, especially in the bus field, and Büssing's best engine is retained in some truck models. This is the 320 horsepower horizontal engine used for the U-series trucks, and was in fact the first six-cylinder engine in Germany to produce the minimum 304 horsepower needed to meet 8 bhp per tonne at 38 tonnes gross. The vertical version of the engine is now discontinued but the horizontal type has a strong following especially among brewery operators. All MANs have the 'Brunswick Lion', which was Büssing's trade mark, on the grille, but those models like the 16.320U which incorporate the Büssing engine have the full name 'MAN Büssing' spelled out on the front of the vehicle. Büssing was one of the greatest names in German automobile engineering dating from the first decade of the 20th century, with some extremely spectacular vehicles over the years. But Büssing is no more, and we have outlined its history in the pictorial sections of this book.

Although Büssing belongs to the past, there is a large and spectacular section of MAN's activity that belongs very much to the future. This is grouped under a general heading of 'new technology', and it is fair to say that MAN has as much if not more experimental work under way to examine new methods of propulsion, construction, control, safety, energy conservation, mass transit of passengers, or indeed any facet of surface transport imaginable, than any other vehicle producer in Europe. The group's involvement in other sectors of industry is, of course, a significant factor in the extent of this research work. For example, MAN builds sections of rocket vehicles for space research, and the metallurgy and cryogenics know-how from that field lends itself to some of the more exotic surface projects, while the advanced electrical technology from the power generation division rubs off in the development of electric vehicles. Consequently a bewildering variety of advanced transport projects emerges from MAN's research workshops. The extent of these would be enough to warrant a special book on its own, but a brief analysis of the most important will serve to illustrate the breadth of activity.

In conjunction with MTU (or Motoren und Turbinen Union) a jointly owned company with Daimler Benz, a gas turbine power programme was launched in the early 1970s. Beginning with a modified helicopter engine, adapted to drive a truck, the engineers gradually developed the technology of heat exchangers and fuel control— necessary for acceptable fuel economy—to a point where a workable turbine truck was a reality. The rapidly spiralling price of oil fuel took the immediacy out of the programme in the mid-1970s, but detail development work is still going on. Like

most other projects at MAN, this one will be stored in the advanced technology archives for use as and when all or part of it can be used in similar or new projects. Another power source on which a great deal of work has been done is that of electrical propulsion, particularly for buses working in dense population areas where pollution factors are critical. A number of designs have been evolved in conjunction with other vehicle and equipment manufacturers. There are 22 of these electric buses running in Düsseldorf and München-Gladbach, working between terminal stations where trailers with freshly charged traction batteries are changed at the end of each trans-city trip. Range is about 90 kilometres on one charge and, of course, the buses are very clean and silent. The whole project is linked with the Dept of New Technology in the German Government, and the Westphalian Land Dept, as a pilot project on where to go when conventional fuels run out. Such a bus could operate from nuclear base-energy obtained through the national electricity grid, and much valuable experience has already been gained.

Another group of projects involves running buses (and trucks) on gas. The first of these was a simple conversion to liquified petroleum gas, butane or propane, similar to many industrial truck applications. This gave a good emissions standard and very good engine life owing to the lack of acidic deposits in the engines. But a far more advanced project was started in 1972 and is still being worked on. That involves the use of natural gas from North Sea wells (or other sources), which gives an extremely clean burning engine, with pollutants only a tiny fraction of those from conventional oil fuels. It is expensive technology, however, because the gas has to be liquified and kept in cryogenic tanks like those on spacecraft. On the other hand there are very real operating advantages, including low fuel cost and excellent environmental habits. A small shift in the price and availability relationship between natural gas and oil fuels would make the system very worthwhile in everyday use, while the concept has real attractions in some oil-producing countries where gas is a waste product.

A continuous programme of automatic vehicle control systems has been going on for about ten years, both for trucks and buses, and the uncanny sight of big vehicles travelling at speed round the Munich test tracks with nobody on board is common these days. The freight vehicle auto-control has applications inside industrial premises rather than on highways, but with passenger vehicles it is a different matter. Two of the problems with bus traffic are the delay caused by other vehicles and the amount of space needed for special tracks. With automatic guidance in dense urban environments, bus tracks could be built in about a third less space, so accurate is the control. A system of guidance has been developed by which the bus is steered by signals from an undersurface cable in city centres and controlled by the driver in the suburbs. Stop-start and door control is permanently under the driver's control at the moment. The system has many advantages for it can work through platform-type bus stops where passengers can walk in one side while others alight opposite, and the guidance is so accurate that prams and shopping carts can be wheeled in and out without trouble, the gap between platform and bus being less than an inch. In new city developments the size of tunnel needed for an underground bus pass is much less than for normal buses or tramcars. This whole system is based on the premise that car traffic has saturated city centres and future passenger expansion will have to be on public transport.

Yet another system under exploration is the stored energy drive, which uses a small diesel engine as basic power, together with a special transmission and a large kinetic flywheel installation. Braking energy and downhill retarding energy is stored in the flywheel and used for accelerating later. There are problems in control at this early stage, but the concept looks feasible and could run a city bus on about half of its present fuel energy consumption. Extensive work has been done on trucks to reduce the amount of energy wasted by moving air about at high speeds. Contoured air shields on top of the cabs, under the nose, behind the cab, on trailer skirts and body corners have shown appreciable savings in total fuel used and from 1978 some of these devices will be available for general sale. The one factor kept in mind in all these experimental projects is cost-effectiveness. The basic rule is that unless any new technology produces a better cost-effectiveness factor than the one that is to be superseded, then it has failed in its aims. Much of the technology needs to be incorporated in long-term planning for city development which is why the work is being done so early in the overall timetable of energy-change patterns. The majority of the work is carried out in conjunction with Germany's Ministry of New Technology.

*     *     *

MAN's trading position as the 1970s draw to a close looks very favourable with a steady and sizeable growth over successive years, averaging about 15 per cent per annum. In money terms, a turnover of Dm 1.7 billion in 1974-75 was boosted to Dm 2.06 billion in 1975-76, and to Dm 2.4 billion in 1976-77. Going back further, to 1972-73, the sales total was only Dm 1.2 billion. Obviously a share of the increase is due to inflation and increased prices, but in fact over five years only 56 per cent of the turnover increase has been due to inflation, the other 46 per cent is an increase in real terms. Taken in numbers of vehicles, the entire production in 1972-3 was 12,000 trucks and 1300 buses and coaches. In 1976-77 the truck total was up to over 17,000 despite the collapse of the German construction vehicle market which comprised between 35 and 40 per cent of MAN's output in the early 1970s. Buses and coaches in the 1976-77 figures doubled from the 1972-73 figures to 2600 of all types. That means that not only did production double in terms of numbers of vehicles since the early 1960s — say 15 years — but the size, complexity and relative value of the typical product increased by approximately 100 per cent in that time.

Otto Voisard, managing director of the MAN Unternehmensbereich Nutzfahrzeuge, or Truck and Bus Division, forecast a continued growth of between 15 and 20 per cent in output over each of the next few years and certainly into the early 1980s at a press conference at the 1977 Frankfurt Show. In addition to that, when the new light-to-medium 'VolksMAN' trucks come on stream in 1980, following their launch at the 1979 Frankfurt Motor Show, an additional 12,000 to 14,000 chassis a year will be added to those totals already quoted. Just how much of that total will go into MAN's account and how much to VW is hard to assess. MAN's responsibility is to make all the engines, front axles and frames, while VW take care of cabs, rear axles and gearboxes, so the nett value is split about 50/50 amounting to an estimated Dm 500 million in the first full year of production. Balanced against that is the loss of the current light truck series, which is essentially the SG-series Saviem with a MAN badge, but as these have not sold well in Germany, that figure will not be large.

A further factor which contributes appreciably to the overall economic picture is the growth in sales of parts, components, and unmachined forgings and castings. The trading position in the late 1970s is illustrated in the table which also shows the values of exported products of all classes. Export figures are quoted with home market figures added in brackets, all in millions of D-marks.

Rates of expansion are expected to continue, some more than others. For example, exports to certain markets like the Middle East will undoubtedly continue to increase to the point where local assembly takes over as it has in India and Gabon. At that point the chassis totals will suffer a downward step, while parts and castings figures will step up correspondingly.

| Products | Trucks | Buses | Engines/axles | Assembly sets to India, Rumania etc | Castings and forgings etc |
|---|---|---|---|---|---|
| 1974-5 | 383(435) | 18(156) | 5(1.6) | 32(nil) | 112(nil) |
| 1975-6 | 399(576) | *146(153) | 6(2.4) | 33(nil) | 129(nil) |
| 1976-7 | 462(818) | 168(142) | 7(3.4) | 35(nil) | 150(nil) |

*includes approximately 100 included under 'trucks' in 1974-5

According to Otto Voisard, MAN as a vehicle producer is stronger in world markets, and at home, than it has been at any time in its history. Obviously exchange rates give rise to a lot of problems, but Voisard looks forward to the day when the Deutsche Mark regains a realistic value in world currency markets, at which point the price-competitiveness position will be much keener than in the late 1970s. As 1978 began, a new assembly line was laid in the Munich works parallel with the original, and that is planned to produce a potential increase of about 60 per cent overall. Corresponding expansion in the Nürnberg engine plant will keep pace with chassis production and increased industrial engine demands. The main motivation for the expansion is the growth of the new industrialisation in African countries and the oil-financed Middle East area, and

to a lesser extent the development of traditional export markets.

A new market emerging as this book is written is in buses for the United States. Following trials of an articulated bus in 1976 by the Urban Mass Transit Authority organisation, orders for over 400 of these very expensive buses have been secured. They are slightly wider than European buses, powered by the turbo-280 D2566 engine and with a small Perkins diesel to drive the air conditioning equipment. These buses are shipped out semi-finished and a contract with American Motors enables that firm to do the detailed finishing to suit individual city and state requirements. The market is expected to grow steadily, and if that is the case, a local assembly operation will be built, just one more in a long list, but a very important one nevertheless.

One of the advanced technology projects closest to the public is the electric bus. In Düsseldorf and München Gladbach 22 of these pollution-free buses went into regular service in 1974. The batteries and regulator gear are contained in a trailer, and changed over at route terminals.

**Above and left** The first prototype four-wheeled turbine truck makes a high speed run in secret in 1971. Five years later sophisticated machines with ceramic heat regenerators were undergoing durability trials on highways at high gross weights.

**Below** A prototype driverless freight vehicle demonstrates its paces on the works track in 1973. The system has applications in internal freight handling systems.

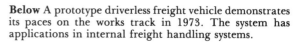

**Above and right** Automatic guidance steers the 'dual mode' bus to within an inch of loading platforms, closer than a driver could steer it. The system is being developed for intensive urban transit systems. The 1978 version is seen in the large picture, the 1972 prototype inset, travelling with no driver.

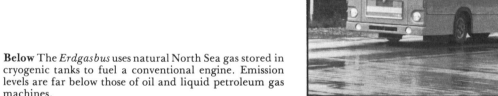

**Below** The *Erdgasbus* uses natural North Sea gas stored in cryogenic tanks to fuel a conventional engine. Emission levels are far below those of oil and liquid petroleum gas machines.

**Above** Aerodynamic research on long-haul trucks has resulted in significant fuel savings at speeds around 80 kph and up.

**Below and right** Spectacular is the only word to describe the performance of the 320 horsepower 8x8 high mobility truck. At right is a military version but civilian types are built in 4x4, 6x6 (below) and 8x8 versions.

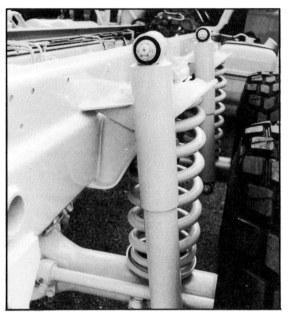

**Left** Advanced suspension design on the high mobility trucks uses long progressive coil springs and very large telescopic dampers.

**Below** Sketches of the new VW-MAN joint light truck exercise show the simple layout and the tilt version of the VW cab. Engines from 90 to 170 horsepower will drive these trucks in the 4.5-14 tonne range.

**Right** The prototype American market articulated bus undergoing operator trials in New York. Over 400 of these extra wide city buses are being supplied to various American city transit authorities. MAN artics have also done trials in Britain.

**Below right** Contrast in size between a 33,000 horsepower ten-cylinder ship's diesel in the erecting shop at Augsburg, and the 280 horsepower D2566 truck engine.

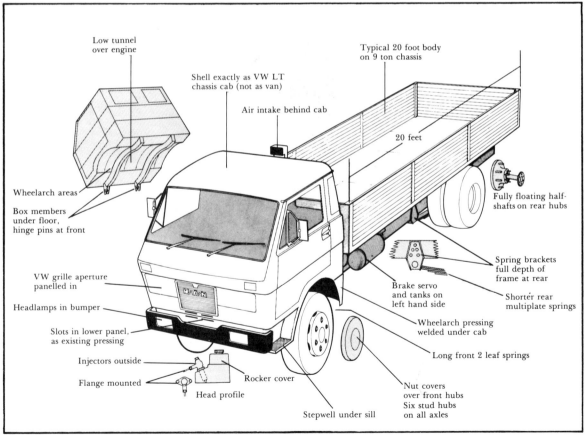

Low tunnel over engine

Shell exactly as VW LT chassis cab (not as van)

Air intake behind cab

Typical 20 foot body on 9 ton chassis

20 feet

Fully floating half-shafts on rear hubs

Wheelarch areas

Box members under floor, hinge pins at front

Spring brackets full depth of frame at rear

Shorter rear multiplate springs

VW grille aperture panelled in

Brake servo and tanks on left hand side

Headlamps in bumper

Wheelarch pressing welded under cab

Slots in lower panel, as existing pressing

Long front 2 leaf springs

Injectors outside

Flange mounted

Rocker cover

Head profile

Nut covers over front hubs Six stud hubs on all axles

Stepwell under sill

**Above** Production US market artic buses use the 280 horsepower horizontal turbocharged D2566 engine, with a Perkins 4-265 diesel to drive the air conditioning plant. This one is on show near Penzburg before shipment to the USA.

**Left and below** Very neat headlamp installation on the 1978 SR coach models employs twin halogen lamps behind a wiped glass screen. Fog lamps fit into the bumper.

Before its take-over by MAN in 1971, the old-established company of Büssing Automobilwerk AG had had a long history of successful engine and vehicle development, particularly in the field of bus transport. The following eleven photographs outline a brief pictorial history of the company's major achievements, beginning (**right**) with this very early Büssing truck with a two-cylinder nine horsepower engine and a 1500 kilograms payload.

**Below** Mechanically operated tipping gear came as a luxury option on trucks from Büssing in 1906.

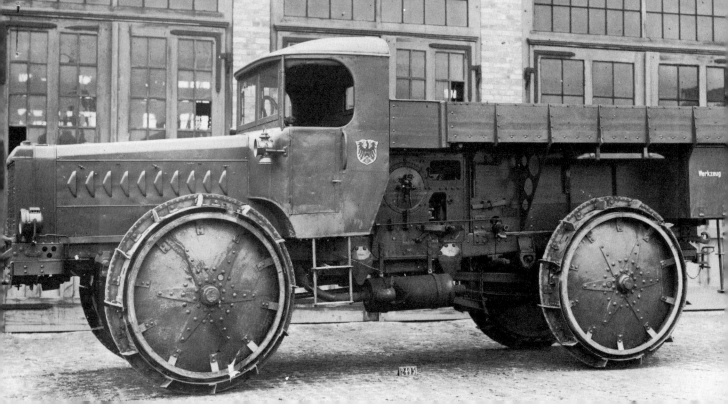

**Left** Büssing-design buses worked with the London General Omnibus Company as early as 1905.

**Below left** This 4ZW heavy military gun tractor was developed for the army during the First World War and had an eight-cylinder petrol engine, shaft drive and an underbody winch.

**Right** Engineering was a Heinrich Büssing forte, and he developed a reliable heavy shaft-drive truck, like this seven ton 50 horsepower type, as early as 1912. The design was widely used by the Reichspost, the German postal authority.

**Below** Long-haul services were operated all over Germany as early as 1926 by Büssing post buses. This very advanced design worked in the Harz mountain area.

**Above and inset right** An interesting concept came from Büssing in 1965, the low-cab *Decklaster*. Some traces of this machine are visible in the X90 project from MAN for the 1990s.

**Below** First 'double-decker' emerged in 1927 and formed the standard type for Berlin for many years.

**Background photograph right** Many of Büssing's designs were spectacular. There was a huge 320 horsepower bus, the 80N, in 1935 with a double-six petrol engine, separate torque-convertor transmissions to the two drive axles, and a top speed of 54 mph.

**Above left** Büssing stayed loyal to petrol engines longer than most. But the diesel was inevitable and they capitulated in style in late 1931 with the FD6 type ten tonner.

**Left** Raba comprises a range of Hungarian-built trucks using a MAN licence. Engines are all from the D21 series.

**Above** The Rumanian-built Roman truck range was introduced to Britain in 1976. This is an R8-135 12 ton model with the 135 horsepower D21 engine and ZF five-speed gearbox.

**Right** Not only Fodens are famous in the band world. MAN have an excellent band seen here welcoming a party of VIPs to the works at Munich. The check pattern flag is that of the state of Bavaria.

**Left** Gräf & Stift is part of the ÖAF group and wholly owned by MAN. This is an artic trollybus, operating in Salzburg in 1975.

**Above** The Austrian-built ÖAF is visually similar to the MAN but uses the older D21 engine range. This one was built with sliding doors and operated for many years hauling trailers loaded with props and costumes at the Austrian State Theatre in Vienna.

**Right** In India the ShaktiMAN (strong MAN) truck production got under way with due ceremony, including lots of flowers in true Indian style.

**Left** Managing director of the vehicle division of MAN during the expansion of the mid-1970s was Otto Voisard, seen here addressing a conference in 1977.

**Below** The X90 project is a 'think exercise' in modular construction. In this long-haul truck, the driving module is atop the sleeping and services module. Identical driving modules are fitted to a variety of trucks, long or short haul. Chassis layout is reminiscent of the Büssing *Decklaster*. The object is to assemble an efficient truck from high-production standard modules, so keeping costs and maintenance problems to a minimum.